Anonymous

The Stonewall Song Book

Being a collection of patriotic, sentimental and comic songs

Anonymous

The Stonewall Song Book
Being a collection of patriotic, sentimental and comic songs

ISBN/EAN: 9783337044558

Printed in Europe, USA, Canada, Australia, Japan

Cover: Foto ©Thomas Meinert / pixelio.de

More available books at **www.hansebooks.com**

Eleventh Edition!---Enlarged!

THE
STONEWALL SONG BOOK,

BEING A

COLLECTION OF PATRIOTIC, SENTIMENTAL

AND

COMIC SONGS.

RICHMOND:

WEST & JOHNSTON.

1865.

STONEWALL SONG BOOK.

Southern Marseillaise.

Sons of the South, awake to glory,
  A thousand voices bid you rise,
Your children, wives, and grandsires hoary,
  Gaze on you now with trusting eyes,
  Gaze on you now with trusting eyes;
Your country every strong arm calling,
  To meet the hireling Northern band,
That comes to desolate the land,
  With fire and blood and scenes appalling.

    To arms, to arms, ye brave,
  The avenging sword unsheathe,
    March on. march on,
  All hearts resolved on victory or death!
    March on, march on,
  All hearts resolved on victory or death!

Now, now the dangerous storm is rolling,
  Which treacherous brothers madly raise,
The dogs of war let loose are howling,
  And soon our peaceful towns may blaze,
  And soon our peaceful towns may blaze;
Shall fiends who basely plot our ruin,
  Unchecke i, advance with guilty stride,.
To spread destruction far and wide,
  With Southrons' blood their hands imbruing?

    To arms, &c.

1

With needy, starving mobs surrounded,
    The jealous, blind fanatics, dare
To offer, in their zeal unbounded,
    Our happy slaves their tender care.
The South, tho' deepest wrongs bewailing,
    Long yielded all to Union's name,
But Independence now we claim,
    And all their threats are unavailing.

    To arms, &c.

The Marseilles Hymn.

Ye sons of France, awake to glory!
    Hark! hark! what myriads bid you rise,
Your children, wives, and grandsires hoary;
    Behold their tears and hear their cries.
Shall hateful tyrants, mischief breeding,
    With hireling host, a ruffian band,
    Affright and desolate the land,
Where peace and liberty lie bleeding?

    To arms, to arms, ye brave,
      The avenging sword unsheathe,
    March on, march on, all hearts resolv'd
      On victory or death!

Now, now the dangerous storm is rolling,
    Which treacherous Kings Confederate raise,
The dogs of war, let loose, are howling,
    And lo! our fields and cities blaze;
And shall we basely view the ruin,
    With lawless force, with guilty stride,
    Spread desolation far and wide,
With crime and blood his hands imbruing?

    To arms, to arms, ye brave, &c.

With luxury and pride surrounded,
    The vile, insatiate despots dare,

Their thirst of power and gold unbound'd,
  To mete and vend the light and air;
Like beasts of burden they wou'd load us,
  Like gods would bid their slaves adore,
But man is man, and who is more?
  Then shall they longer lash and goad us?

To arms, to arms, ye brave, &c.

Oh! Liberty! can man resign thee,
  Once having felt thy generous flame?
Can dungeons, bolts or bars confine thee?
  Or whips thy noble spirit tame?
Too long the world has wept bewailing
  That falsehood's dagger tyrants wield,
But freedom is our sword and shield,
  And all their arts are unavailing.

To arms, to arms, ye brave, &c.

Ever of Thee.

Ever of thee I'm fondly dreaming,
  Thy gentle voice my spirit it can cheer;
Thou wert the star that, mildly beaming,
  Shone o'er my path when all was dark and drear.
Still in my heart thy form I cherish;
  Every kind thought. like a bird, flies to thee;
Ah! never, till life and memory perish,
  Can I forget how dear thou art to me.
    Morn, noon and night, where'er I may be,
    Fondly I'm dreaming ever of thee,
    Fondly I'm dreaming ever of thee.

Ever of thee, when sad and lonely,
  Wandering afar my soul joy'd to dwell;
Ah! then I felt I loved thee only;
  All seem'd to fade before affection's spell).
Years have not chill'd the love I cherish,
  True as the stars has my heart been to thee.
Ah! never, till life and memory perish,
  Can I forget, &c.

The Irish Jaunting Car.

Air—BONNIE BLUE FLAG.

Do you want a car, yer honor? Och! sure that's the
    one for you;
It's an outside Irish Jaunting Car, just painted green
    and blue; .
It belongs to Larry Doolan, and you'll have to travel
    far
To find a better driver of an Irish Jaunting Car.
The fare is fifteen pence, but as the distance isn't far,
I'll just say one and three pence, Ma'am, so jump upon
    the car.

If you want to drive 'round Dublin, sure, you'll find
    me on the strand,
I'll take you to Raheny, to pick cockles on the strand!
To the Phœnix Park, to Nancy Hands, the Monument,
    and then
I'll take you to the Strawberry Beds, and back to town
    again.
Get some bread and beef and porter, and some whiskey
    in a jar,
That's the way to take your pleasure on an Irish
    Jaunting Car.

Oh! then if that car should speak, Sir, sure a moral
    'twould disclose,
It has carried Whigs and Tories, Repealers and their
    foes;
Yet it looks well by obliging all, and keeps me better
    far,
With my whip, my pipe, my pony, and my Irish Jaunt-
    ing Car,
So if you want to hire me, call into Mr. Mahar,
And he'll send for Larry Doolan and his Irish Jaunt-
    ing Car.

Annie Laurie.

Maxwelton Braes are bonnie,
  Where early fa's the dew,
And it's there that Annie Laurie
  Gie'd me her promise true,
  Gie'd me her promise true,
Which ne'er forgot will be,
  And for bonnie Annie Laurie
I'd lay me down and dee.

Her brow is like the snow drift,
  Her throat is like the swan,
Her face it is the fairest
  That e'er the sun shone on—
  That e'er the sun shone on;
And dark blue is her e'e,
  And for bonnie Annie Laurie
I'd lay me down and dee.

Like dew on the gowan lying,
  Is the fa' o' her fairy feet,
And like the winds in summer sighing,
  Her voice is low and sweet—
  Her voice is low and sweet,
And she's a' the world to me;
  And for bonnie Annie Laurie
I'd lay me down and 'dee.

Nelly Gray.

There's a low green valley on the old Kentucky shore,
  Where I've whiled many happy hours away,
A sitting and a singing by the little cottage door,
  Where lived my darling Nelly Gray.

CHORUS—Oh! my poor Nelly Gray,
      They have taken you away,
  And I'll never see my darling any more;
    I'm sitting by the river,
    And I'm weeping all the day,
  For you've gone from Old Kentucky shore.

When the moon had climbed the mountain, and the
    stars were shining too,
Then I'd take my darling Nelly Gray,
And we'd float down the river in my little canoe,
    While my banjo sweetly I wou'd play.
        Chorus—Oh! my poor Nelly Gray, &c.

One night I went to see her, but she's gone, the neigh-
    bors say,
    The white man bought her for his gain,
They have taken her to Georgia for to wear her life
    away,
    As she toils in the cotton and the cane.
        Chorus—Oh! my poor Nelly Gray, &c.

My canoe is under the water, and my banjo is unstrung,
    I'm tired of living any more :
My eyes shall look downward, and my songs shall be
    unsung,
    While I stay on the Old Kentucky shore
        Chorus—Oh! my poor Nelly Gray, &c.

My eyes are getting blinded, and I cannot see my way.
    Hark! there's somebody knocking at the door;
Oh! I hear the angels calling, and I see my Nelly Gray;
    Farewell to the Old Kentucky shore.

        Chorus—Oh! my darling Nelly Gray,
                Up in heaven there they say,
        That they will never take you from me any more.
        I'm a coming, coming, coming,
            As the angels clear the way;
        Farewell to the Old Kentucky shore.

Cottage by the Sea.

Childhood's days now pass before me,
    Forms and scenes of long ago,
Like a dream they hover o'er me,
    Calm and bright as the evening's glow;

Days that knew no shade of sorrow,
  When my young heart, pure and free,
Joyful hailed each coming morrow,
  In the cottage, the cottage by the sea—
Joyful hailed each coming morrow,
  In the cottage, the cottage by the sea.

Fancy sees the rose-trees twining
  Round the old and rustic door,
And below the white beach shining,
  Where I gathered shells of yore;
Hears my mother's gentle warning,
  As she took me on her knee,
And I feel again life's morning,
  In the cottage, the cottage by the sea.

What though years have roll'd above me,
  Though 'mid fairer scenes I roam,
Yet I ne'er shall cease to love thee,
  Childhood's dear and happy home;
And when life's long day is closing,
  Oh! how pleasant would it be,
On some faithful breast reposing,
  In the cottage by the sea—
On some faithful breast reposing,
  In the cottage, the cottage by the sea.

The Original Home, Sweet Home.

BY JOHN HOWARD PAYNE.

'Mid pleasures and palaces, though we may roam,
Be it ever so humble, there is no place like home;
A charm from the skies seems to hallow us there,
Which, seek through the world, is ne'er met with
    elsewhere.
    Home, home, sweet, sweet home,
      There's no place like home—
      There's no place like home.

I gazed on the moon as I traced the drear wild,
And feel that my parent now thinks on her child;
She looks on that moon from her own cottage door,
Through woodbines, whose fragrance shall cheer me
no more.
Home, home, &c.

An exile from home, sp'endor dazzles in vain,
Oh! give me my lonely thatch'd cottage again;
The birds singing gaily. that came at my call,
Give me them, with a peace of mind, dearer than all.
Home, home, sweet, sweet home.

Kate Kearney.

Oh! did you not hear of Kate Kearney?
She lives on the banks of Killarney,
From the glance of her eye,
Shun danger and fly.
For fatal's the glance of Kate Kearney.

For that eye is so modestly beaming,
You'd ne'er think of mischief she's dreaming,
Yet, oh! I can tell
How fatal's the spell
That lurks in the eye of Kate Kearney.

Oh! should you e'er meet this Kate Kearney,
Who lives on the banks of Killarney,
Beware of her smile,
For many a wile
Lies hid in the smile of Kate Kearney.

Though she looks so bewitchingly simple,
There's mischief in every dimple;
And who dares inhale
Her sigh's spicy gale,
Must die by the breath of Kate Kearney.

Answer to Kate Kearney.

Oh! yes. I have seen this Kate Kearney,
Who lives near the lake of Killarney;
   From her love-beaming eye,
   Wha mortal can fly.
Unsubdued by the glance of Kate Kearney?

For that eye so seducingly meaning,
Assures me of mischief she's dreaming;
   And I feel 'tis in vain
   To fly from the chain
That binds me to lovely Kate Kearney.

At eve when I've met this Kate Kearney,
On the flow'r-mantled banks of Killarney,
   Her smile would impart
   Thrilling joy to my heart,
As I gazed on the charming Kate Kearney.

On the banks of Killarney reclining,
My bosom to rapture resigning,
   I've felt the keen smart
   Of love's fatal dart,
And inhal'd the warm sigh of Kate Kearney.

―――――❖❖❖―――――

The Last Rose of Summer

'Tis the last rose of summer,
   Left blooming alone,
All her lovely companions
   Are faded and gone;
No flow'r of her kindred,
   No rosebud is nigh,
To reflect back her blushes,
   Or give sigh for sigh!

I'll not leave thee, thou lone one,
   To pine on the stem,

Since the lovely are sleeping,
  Go sleep thou with them;
Thus kindly I'll scatter
  Thy leaves o'er thy bed,
Where thy mates of the garden
  Lie scentless and dead.

So soon may I follow,
  When friendships decay,
And from Love's shining circle
  The gems drop away;
When true hearts lie wither'd,
  And fond ones are flown,
O! who would inhabit
  This bleak world alone?

Round.

(*For four Voices.*)

Scotland's burning! Scotland's burning!
  Look out! Look out!
Fire! Fire! Fire! Fire! Fire! Fire!
Cast on water! Cast on water!

The Mocking Bird.

I'm dreaming now of Allie, sweet Allie, sweet Allie,
    I'm dreaming now of Allie,
For the thought of her is one that never dies,
She is sleeping in the valley, the valley, the valley—
    She's sleeping in the valley,
And the mocking bird is singing where she lies;
    Listen to the mocking bird,
    Listen to the mocking bird.
The mocking bird still singing o'er her grave;
    Listen to the mocking bird,
    Listen to the mocking bird,
Still singing where the weeping willows wave.

Ah! well I yet remember, remember, remember,
   Ah! well I yet remember,
When we gather'd in the cotton side by side,
'Twas in the mild September September, September,
  ' 'Twas in the mild September,
And the mocking bird was singing far and wide :
    Listen to the mocking bird,
    Listen to the mocking bird,
The mocking bird still singing o'er her grave :
    Listen to the mocking bird,
    Listen to the mocking bird,
Still singing where the weeping willows wave.

When the charms of spring awaken, awaken, awaken,.
   When the charms of spring awaken,
And the mocking bird is singing on the bough,
I feel like one forsaken, forsaken, forsaken,
   I feel like one forsaken,
Since my Allie is no longer with me now;
    Listen to the mocking bird,
    Listen to the mocking bird,
The mocking bird still singing o'er her grave;
    Listen to the mocking bird,
    Listen to the mocking bird,
Still singing where the weeping willows wave.

Fairy Belle.

The pride of the village, and the fairest in the dell,
Is the queen of my song, and her name is Fairy Belle;
The sound of her light steps may be heard upon the
    hill,
Like the fall of the snow drop or the dripping of the
    rill.

CHORUS.

Fairy Belle, gentle Fairy Belle,
   The star of the night and the lily of the day,
Fairy Belle, the queen of all the dell,
   Long may she revel on her bright sunny way.

She sings to the meadows, and she carols to the
    streams,
She laughs in the sunlight, and smiles while in her
    dreams;
Her hair. like the thistle down, is borne upon the air,
And her heart. like the humming bird's, is free from
    every care.
        Chorus—Fairy Belle, &c.

Her soft notes of melody around me sweetly fall,
Her eyes, full of love. is now beaming on my soul;
The sound of that gentle voice, the glance of that eye,
Surround me with rapture that no other heart could
    sigh.
        Chorus—Fairy Belle, &c.

The Lisping Lover.

Have you e'er been in love? if you haven't, I have;
To the mighty God Koopid I've been a great thlave,
He thot in my huthom a quiver of harrows,
Like naughty boys thoot at cock robins and thparrows.
My heart was as pure as the white alabather,
Till Koopid my huthom weak d d overmather;
Then ye gods only know how I lov'd one Mith Julia,
There was thomething about her tho wery pekooliar!
(Spoken)   Wery, wery pekooliar indeed!
There was thomething about her tho wery pekooliar!

We met first at a Ball, where our hands did entwine,
And I d d thqueedge her finger and she did thqueedge
    mine,
To be my next partner I ventured to preth her,
And I found that she lithp'd when she answered me
    ' ye h thir '
Now in lithping I think there is thomething uncom-
    mon,
I love in partiklar a lithp in an ooman;
I'm thure you d have lik'd the lithp of Mith Julia,
There was thomething ab ut it tho wery pekooliar!
(Spoken)   Wery pekooliar! wery pekooliar indeed!
There was thomething about it tho wery pekooliar!

Like a beautiful peach was the cheek of my Ju'ia,
And then in her eye there was thomething pekooliar;
Speaking wolumes, it darted each glance to one's mar-
    row,
As thwill and as keen as the wicked boy's harrow.
A thlight catht in her eye to her looks added wigor;
A catht in the eye often tends to disfigure,
But not tho the catht in the eye of Miss Julia,
There was thomething about it tho wery pekooliar!
(*Spoken.*) Wery pekooliar! wery pekooliar indeed!
There was thomething about it tho wery pekooliar!

Good friends were we thoon, and 'midst thmiles and
    'midst tears,
I courted her nearly for three or four years.
I took her to plays and balls—Oh! ye powers!
How thweetly and thwitly did then path my hours:
But once—oh! e'en now I my feelingth can't thmother,
She danced all the evening along with another.
I didn't thay nothing that night to Mith Julia,
But I couldn't help thinking 'twas wery pekooliar!
(*Spoken*) Wery pekooliar, wery pekooliar indeed; thir!
Yeth, I couldn't help thinking 'twas wery pekooliar!

I went next day to thcold, when she to my heart's core
Cut me up by requething I'd come there no more,
And I thould be affronted if longer I tarried,
For next week to another she was to be married.
Gods, Julia! thaid I, you do not thay so?
"Yeth, but I do, thir, tho you'd better go."
Well, I thall go, but surely you'll own it, Mith Julia,
Your behavior to me hath been wery pekooliar?
Tho from that day to this I have never theen Julia,
Her behavier to me wath tho wery pekooliar!

---❧---

Dinna Forget.

Dinna forget, laddie, dinna forget,
Ne'er make me rue that we have ever met :
Wide tho' we sever, parted forever,
Willie, when far away, dinna forget.

We part, and it may be we meet never mair,
Yet my heart, as in Hope, will be true in despair,
And the sigh of remembrance, the tear of regret,
For thee will be frequent; then dinna forget.

When the star o'er the gloaming' is beaming above
Think how oft it hath lighted the tryst of our love;
Oh! deem it an angel's e'e heaven hath set
To watch thee, to warn thee, sae dinnu forget.

Home--A Ballad!

The dearest spot of earth to me
  Is home, sweet home!
The fairy land I long to see
  Is home, sweet home!
There how charmed the sense of hearing,
There where love is so endearing,
All the world is not so cheering
  As home, sweet home!
The dearest spot of earth to me
  Is home, sweet home!
The fairy land I long to see
  Is home, sweet home!

I've taught my heart the way to prize
  My home, sweet home!
I've learned to look with lover's eyes
  On home, sweet home!
There, where vows are truly plighted,
There, where hearts are so united,
All the world besides I've slighted
  For home, sweet home!
The dearest spot of earth to me.
  Is home, sweet home!
The fairy land I long to see
  Is home, sweet home!

The Musical Cat.

The cat came out from under the barn,
With a fiddle-stick under his arm,
And all the tune that he could play,
Was "over the hills and far away."
Over the hills, and a great way off,
Where 'po-sums die of the whooping cough!—
Over the hills, and a great way off,
Where possums die of the whooping cough!
[This was the last ever heard of the *mew*-sical cat.]

———♦♦♦———

[From the Southern Illustrated News.]

Richmond's A Hard Road to Travel;

*Or the New Jordan, as sung with enthusiastic applause in
all the Northern Theatres.*

Would you like to hear the song, I'm afraid its rather
    long,
Of the famous "On to Richmond" double trouble—
Of the half-a-dozen slips, on a half-a-dozen trips,
    And the very latest bur-ting of the bubble?
Then list while I relate this most unhappy fate,
    'Tis a dreadful knotty puzzle to unravel,
Though all the papers swore, when we touched Vir-
    ginia's shore,
 ' That Richmond was an easy road to travel :   •
    Then pull off your coat and roll up your sleeve,
    For Richmond's a hard road to travel :
    Then pull off your coat, and roll up your sleeve,
    For Richmond's a hard road to travel I believe.

First McDowell, bold and gay, set forth the shortest
    way
    By Manassas in the pleasant summer weather,
But he quickly went and ran on a Stonewall, foolish
    man,

And had a "rocky" journey altogether;
For he found it rather hard to ride over Beauregard,
And Johnston proved a deuce of a bother,
And 'twas clear, beyond a doubt, that he didn't like
the *rout*,
And a second time would have to try another:
Then pull off your coat, and roll up your sleeve,
For Richmond's a hard road to travel;
Manassas gave us fits, and Bull Run it made us
grieve,
Oh! Richmond's a hard road to travel I believe.

Next came the Woolly Horse, with an overwhelming
force,
To march down to Richmond by the Valley,
But he couldn't find the road, and his "onward move-
ment" showed
His campaigning was a mere shilly-shally.
And Commissary Banks, with his motley foreign ranks,
The Dutchman and the Celt, not the Saxon,
Lost the whole of his supplies, and with tears in his
eyes,
Ran away from that dunder-headed Jackson:
Then pull off your coat, and roll up your sleeve,
For Richmond's a hard road to travel;
The Valley wouldn't do, as everybody knows,
And Richmond's a hard road to travel I suppose.

Then the great Galena came, with her port-holes all
aflame,
And the Monitor, that famous naval wonder,
But the guns at Drewry's Bluff, gave them speedily
enough
Of the loudest sort of real rebel thunder:
The Galena was astonished, and the Monitor admon-
ished
And their efforts to ascend the stream was mocked
at,
While the dreadful Naugatuck, by the hardest kind of
luck,
Was very nearly knocked into a cocked hat.

Then pull off your coat, and roll up your sleeves,
  For·Richmond's a hard road to travel;
The gunboats gave it up in a stupefied despair,
  And Richmond is a hard road to travel, I declare.

Then McClellan followed soon, with spade and with
    balloon,
  To try the Peninsular approaches,
But one and all agreed, that his best rate of speed
  Wasn't faster than the slowest of "slow coaches :"
Instead of easy ground, at Williamsburg he found
  A LONG STREET indeed, and nothing shorter,
And it put him in the dumps, that spades wasn't trumps,
  And the HILLS he couldn't level as he "orter :"
    Then pull off your coat and roll up your sleeve,
      For Richmond's a hard to travel;
    Lay down the shovel, and fling away the spade,
      For Richmond's a hard road to travel I'm afraid.

He tried the rebel lines, on the field of Seven Pines,
  Where his troops did such awful heavy chargin',
But he floundered in the mud, and he saw a stream of
    blood
  Over the Chickahominy's sweet margin;
Though the fact seems rather strange, when he left his
    gunboats' range,
  On land he drifted overmuch to LEE-ward,
So he quickly "changed his base," in a sort of steeple-
    chase,
  And hurried back to Stanton, Abe and Seward :
    Then pull off your coat, and roll up your sleeve,
      For Richmond's a hard road to travel;
    We shouldn't be surprised that McClellan took to
      drinking,
    For Richmond's a hard road to travel I'm a
      thinking.

Then said Lincoln unto Pope, "You can make the trip
    I hope :"
  Quoth the bragging Major-General, "Yes, that I
    can,"

And began to issue orders to his terrible marauders,
  Just like another Leo of the Vatican;
But that same demented Jackson, this fellow laid his
  whacks on,
  And made him by compulsion a Seceder,*
And Pope took a rapid flight from Manassas' second
  fight,
  'Twas his very last appearance as a leader :
    Then pull off your coat, and roll up your sleeve,
    For Richmond's a hard road to travel;
  Pope tried his very best, and was evidently sold,
    And Richmond's a hard road to travel I am told.

Last of all the brave Burnside, with his pontoon
  bridges tried
A road no one had thought of before him,
With two hundred thousand men for the rebel "slaugh-
  ter pen,"
And the blessed Union flag a flying o'er him;
But he met a "fire of hell," of canister and shell,
  Enough to make the knees of any man knock;
'Twas a shocking sight to view, that second Waterloo,
  On the banks of the pleasant Rappahannock :
    Then pull off your coat, and roll up your sleeve,
    For Richmond's a hard road to travel;
  'Twas a shocking sight to view, that second Wa-
    terloo,
    And Richmond's a bloody road to travel it is true.

We are very much perplexed to know who will try it
  next,
  And to guess by what new high road he *may* go,
But the Capital must blaze, and that in ninety days,
  For 'tis written *Delenda est Carthago.*
We'll take the cursed town, and then we'll burn it
  down,
  And plunder and hang up every rebel;
Yet the contraband was right, when he told us they
  would fight—
    "O yis, marsa, they'll fight like the debble."

* See Cedar (*Run.*)·

Then pull off your coat and roll up your sleeve
For Richmond's a hard road to travel;
We've played our strongest card, and 'tis plain
     that we are slammed,
And if Richmond ain't a hard road to travel,
I'll be —— blamed.

The Harp that Once through Tara's Halls.

The harp that once thro' Tara's halls
     The soul of music shed,
Now hangs as mute on Tara's walls
As if that soul were fled:
So sleeps the pride of former days,
     So glory's thrill is o'er,
And hearts that once beat high for praise
     Now feel that praise no more.

No more the chiefs and ladies bright
     The Harp of Tara swells,
The chord alone that breaks at night
     Its tale of ruin tells.
Thus freedom now so seldom wakes,
     The only throb she gives
Is when some heart indignant breaks
     To show that still she lives.

Hazel Dell.

In the Hazel Dell my Nelly's sleeping
     Nelly loved so long.
And my lonely, lonely watch I'm keeping,
     Nelly lost and gone:
Here in moonlight often have we wandered
     Thro' the silent shade,
Now where leafy branches drooping downward,
     Little Nelly's laid.

CHORUS.—All alone my watch I'm keeping
    In the Hazel Dell,
    For my darling Nelly is near me sleeping,
    Nelly, dear, farewell.

In the Hazel Dell my Nelly's sleeping,
    Where the flowers wave,
And the silent stars are nightly weeping
    O'er poor Nelly's grave.
Hopes that once my bosom fondly cherished
    Smile no more for me,
Since my darling Nelly perished,
    Nelly, I come to thee.

CHORUS.—All alone, &c.

---◆◆◆---

Happy are We To-Night.

Happy are we to-night, boys,
    Happy, happy are we;
The hearts that we delight, boys,
    With us may happy be.
Friends should laugh with those who laugh,
    And sigh for those in pain,
The most of us have met before,
    And now we meet again.

CHORUS.—Happy are we to-night, boys,
    Happy, happy are we;
    The hearts that we delight, boys,
    With us may happy be.

Many will be the mile, boys,
    Many, many the mile
That we shall rove and smile, boys,
    With friends we ne'er beguile.
The voices we have often heard,
    And faces we have often met,
Like tones of sweetest melody,
    We never can forget.

CHORUS.—Happy are we, &c.

Weary we may return, boys,
  Weary, weary at last;
But memory will learn, boys,
  To love the happy past.
Age may bring us gloomy hours,
  And time may make us sad,
But we to-night are free from care,
  And all our hearts are glad.

CHORUS.—Happy are we, &c.

The Bachanalians.

[OLD SONG.]]

CHORUS.—Come, landlord, fill your flowing bowl,
  Until it doth run over,
  For to-night we'll merry, merry be,
  To-morrow we'll get sober.

SOLO.—The man that drinks good brandy, O,
  And goes to bed mellow,
Lives as he ought to live,
  And dies a clever fellow.

CHORUS.—Come, landlord, &c.

The man that drinks water, boys,
  And goes to bed sober,
Falls as the leaves do fall,
  And dies in October.

CHORUS.—Come, landlord, &c.

But he who drinks just what he wants,
  And getteth half seas over,
Will live until he dies, perhaps;
  And then lie down in clover.

CHORUS.—Come, landlord, &c,

Nae Luck about the House.

["This," says Burns, "is one of the most beautiful songs in the Scott or any other language." The authorship is ascribed to a poor schoolmistress, named Joan Adams, who lived in Grenock early in the last century. The song, as now published, has been somewhat anglicised and abridged.]

And are ye sure the news is true?
And are ye sure he's weel?
Is this a time to think of work?
Ye jauds, throw by your wheel.
Is this the time to think of work,
When Colin's at the door?
Reach my cloak, I'll to the quay,
And see him come ashore.
 For there's nae luck about the house,
  There's nae luck at a',
  There's little pleasure in the house
  When our gudeman's awa'.

And gi'e to me higgonet,
My bishop's satin gown,
For I must tell the bailie's wife
That Colin's come to town.
My turkey slippers must go on,
My hose o' pearly blue,
'Tis a' to please my own gudeman,
For he's both leal and true.
 For there's nae luck, &c.

So true his heart, so kind his speech,
His breath like caller air,
His very foot has music in't
As he comes up the stair.
And will I see his face again?
And will I hear him speak?
I'm downright dizzy wi' the thought,
In troth I'm like to greet. (Cry.)
 For there's nae luck, &c.

The cold blast of the winter wind,
　That thrilled through my heart,
They are blown by—I have him safe,
　Till death we'll ne'er part;
But what pu's parting in my head?
　It may be far awa';
The present moment is our own,
　The next we never saw.
　　　For there's nae luck, &c.

Since Colin's well, I'm well content,
　I have no more to crave;
Could I but live to make him blest,
　I'm blest above the lave.
And will I see his face again?
　And will I hear him speak?
I'm downright dizzy wi' the thought,—
　For there's nae luck, &c.

The Stars and the Bars.

Above us our banner is waving,
　The hope of the brave and the free;
We must watch, must guard and defend it,
　'Till the minions of tyranny flee;
With swords and good rifles we'll meet them
　On the hill, the vale and the plain,
And though they may come like the locusts,
　We'll fatten our land with their slain.

　　Then shout for the stars and the bars,
　　Three cheers for the bars and the stars;
　　A nation has sworn to defend them,
　　They'll die for the stars and bars.

Brave sons of the South are now ready,
　Each bosom is burning to save
Our land of bright sunshine and flower,
　From the tread of the Northern slave.

And mothers, though bending in anguish,
  Thus nobly cry out to their sons,
"Go, meet the invader with firmness,
  And true be the aim of your guns."
     Then shout, &c.

Far better to live in a desert,
  The blue sky our canopy too—
Than wearing the chains of these demons,
  The selfish fanatic'd crew.
Far better to perish with honor;
  Far better to go to the grave,
And better to *die* as a freeman
  Than live as a Northerner's slave.
     Then shout, &c.

The Captain.

As they marched through the town with their banners
    so gay,
I ran to the window just to hear the band play;
I peeped through the blinds very cautiously then,
Lest the neighbors should say that I looked at the men
Oh! I heard the drums beat, and the music so sweet,
But my eyes at that moment had a much greater treat,
The troop was the finest I ever did see,
And the Captain with his whiskers took a sly glance
    at me.

When we met at the ball; I, of course, thought 'twas
    right
To pretend that we never had met till that night;
But he knew me at once, I peceived by his glance,
And I looked down and blushed when he asked me to
    to dance,
Oh! he sat by my side at the end of the set,
And the sweet words he spoke I never can forget,
For my heart was enlisted, and could not get free,
As the Captain with his whiskers took a sly glance
    at me.

But he marched from the town, and I see him no more,
Yet I think of him oft, and the whiskers he wore;
I dream all the night and talk all the day
Of the love of a Captain who went far away.
I remember with superabundant delight
When we met in the street, and we danced all the
  night,
And keep in my mind how my heart jumped with glee
As the Captain with his whiskers took a sly glance at
  me.

But there's hope, for a friend, just ten minutes ago,
Said the Captain's returned from the war, and I know
He'll be searching for me with considerable zest,
And when I'm found—but ah! you know all the rest
Perhaps he is here—let me look round the house—
Be still every one of you, as still as a mouse
For if the dear creature is here, he will be
With his whiskers a taking sly glances at me.

————◆◆◆————

Round.

[*For three Voices.*]

A boat! a boat! to cross the ferry,
And we'll go over to be merry,
To laugh and quaff, and drink good sherry.

————◆◆◆————

The Conscript's Departure.

You are going far away, far away from your Jeannette,
There is no one left to love me now, and you, too, may
  forget,
But my heart it will be with you wherever you may go,
Can you look me in the face and say the same, Jeannot?
When you wear the jacket red, and the beautiful cock-
  ade,

Oh! I fear you will forget all the promises you made,
With the gun upon your shoulder, and the bayonet by
  your side,
You'll be taking some proud lady and be making her
  your bride,
        You'll be taking some, &c.

Or when glory leads the way, you'll be madly rushing
  on,
Never thinking if they kill you that my happiness is
  gone,
If you win the day, perhaps a General you'll be,
Tho' I'm proud to think of that, what will become of
  me?
Oh! if I were Queen of France, or still better, Pope
  of Rome,
I would have no fighting men abroad, and weeping
  maids at home,
All the world should be at peace, or if king's must
  show their might,
Why let those who make the quarrels be the only men
  who fight;
        Yes, let those who make the quarrels, &c.

----◆●◆----

Emma Jane.

'Tis of a young maiden that a story I'll tell,
Also of her lovieur, and what them befell,
Oh! her lovieur was a salieur, he sailed the salt sea,
And the consequences attending his parting from she.
        And the consequences, &c.

Oh! the vessel of the Captain was called the Emma
  Jane,
And in honor of his true love the Captain gave her
  that name,
But he never more was heard of, nor his vessel so brave,
And 'twas calculated pretty generally she found a wa-
  tery grave—
        And 'twas calculated, &c.

On a cold stone all summer, by the side of the sea,
This maiden kept a watching; and awaiting for he,
Till on one cold frosty morning in the water she was
 found.
And it was calculated, pretty generally, she got crazy
 and was drowned.

Now just two years after these ere events occurred,
A stranger came to the town where Emma Jane was
 buried,
He axed of the Sexting where Emma Jane might be,
And he answered by pinting towards the willer tree.

Now they buried the body of the Captain close by her,
And over his tomb they set out a green brier,
So the willer tree a weepin' is an emblem of she,
And the brier clingin' round is an emblem of he.

Bonny Eloise.

Oh! sweet is the vale where the Mohawk gentle glides
 On its clear winding way to the sea,
And dearer than all storied streams on earth besides
 Is this bright rolling river to me;
  But sweeter, dearer, yes dearer far than those,
   Who charms where others all fail,
  Is blue-eyed bonny, bonny Eloise,
  The belle of the Mohawk vale.

Oh! sweet are the scenes of my boyhood's sunny years
 That bespangle the gay valley o'er,
And dear are the friends seen thro' memory's fond
 tears,
 That have lived in the blest days of yore;
  But sweeter, dearer, &c.

Oh! sweet are the moments when dreaming I roam
 Thro' my loved haunts now mossy and grey;
And dearer than all is my childhood's hallow'd home,
 That is crumbling now slowly away;
  But sweeter, dearer, &c;

Root Hog or Die.

THE CAMP VERSION.

Old Abe Lincoln keeps kicking up a fuss,
I think he'd better stop it, for he'll only make it worse,
We'll have our independence, I'll tell you the reason
    why,
Jeff. Davis will make them sing, "Root hog or die."

When Lincoln went to reinforce Sumter for the fight,
He told his men to pass through the harbor in the
    night,
He said to them be careful, I'll tell you the reason why,
The Southern boys are mighty bad on "Root hog or
    die.

Then Beauregard called a halt, according to the style,
The Lincolnites faced about and looked mighty wild,
They cou'd'nt give the password, I'll tell you the rea-
    son why,
Beauregard's countersign was "Root hog or die:"

They anchored out a battery upon the waters free,
It was the queerest looking thing that ever you did see;
It was th' fall of Sumter, I'll tell you the reason why,
It was the Southern alphabet of "Root hog or die."

They telegraphed to Abraham they took her like a flirt,
They understood another line, "there was nobody
    hurt,"
We are bound to have the Capitol, I'll tell you the
    reason why,
We want to teach Old Abe to sing, "Root hog or die."

When Abram read the dispatch the tear came in his
    eye,
He wal'ed his eyes to Bobby, and Bob began to cry,
They prayed to Jeff. to spare them, I'll tell you the
    reason why,
They did'nt want to "mark time" to "Root hog or
    die."

The "Kentucky braves" at Trenton are eager for the
    fight,
They want to help the Southern boys set Old Abra'm
    right;
They had to leave their native State, I'll tell you the
    reason why,
Old Kentucky would'nt sing, "Root hog or die."

The New Yankee Doodle.

Yankee Doodle had a mind
    To whip the Southern traitors,
Because they did'nt choose to live
    On codfish and potatoes.
      Yankee Doodle, doodle doo,
        Yankee Doodle dandy,
      And so to keep his courage up,
      He took a drink of brandy.

Yankee Doodle drew his sword,
    And practiced all the passes;
Come, boys we'll take another drink
    When we get to Manassas.
      Yankee Doodle, doodle doo,
        Yankee Doodle dandy,
      They never reached Manassas plain,
      And never got the brandy.

Yankee Doodle, oh! for shame,
    You're always intermeddling;
Let guns alone, they're dangerous things,
    You'd better stick to pudding.
      Yankee Doodle, doodle doo,
        Yankee Doodle dandy.
      When next you go to Bully Run,
      You'll throw away the brandy.

On to Glory.

Sons of Freedom! on to glory!
  Go where brave men to or die,
Let your names in future story
  Gladden every patriot's eye:
'Tis your country calls you, hasten!
  Backward hurl the invading foe:
Freemen! never think of danger,
  To the glorious battle go.

Oh! remember gallant Jackson, ·
  Single-handed in the fight,
Death blows dealt the fierce marauder,
  For his liberty and right.
Tho' he fell beneath their thousands,
  Who that covets not his fame?
Grand and glorious, brave and noble,
  Henceforth shall be Jackson's name.

Sons of Freedom! can you linger,
  When you hear the battle's roar,
Fondly dallying with your pleasures
  When the foe is at your door!
Never, no! we fear no idlers,
  "Death or Freedom's" now the cry
Till the STARS and BARS triumphant
  Spread their folds to every eye.

Villikins and His Dinah.

'Tis of a rich merchant who in London did dwell,
He had but one daughter, an uncommon nice young gal,
Her name it was Dinah, scarce sixteen years old,
With a very large fortune of silver and gold.
    Singing to la lol la rol rol to ral lal la.

As Dinah was walking the garden one day,
Her papa he came to her and thus he did say,
"Go dress yourself, Dinah, in gorgeous array,
And take yourself a husband both gallant and gay."
Singing, &c.

"Oh! papa, oh! papa, I've not made up my mind,
And to marry jus yet, why I don't feel inclined;
To you my large fortune I'll gladly give o'er,
If you'll let me live single a year or two more."
Singing, &c.

"Go, go, boldest daughter," the parient replied,
"If you won't consent to be this young man's bride;
I'll give your large fortune to the nearest of kin,
And you shan't reap the benefit of one single pin."
Singing, &c.

As Villikins was a walking the garden around,
He spied his dear Dinah lying dead upon the ground,
And the cup of cold pison it lay by her side,
And a billet-doux a stating 'twas by pison she died.
Singing, &c.

He kissed her cold corpus a thousand times o'er,
And called her his Dinah, though she was no more.
Then swallowed the pison like a lovyer so brave,
And Villikins and his Dinah lie both in one grave.
Singing, &c.

MORAL.

Now all you young maidens take warning by her,
Never, not by no means, disobey your governor;
And all you young fellows mind who you clap eyes on,
Think of Villikins and Dinah and the cup of cold pison.
Singing, &c.

Oft in the Stilly Night.

Oft in the stilly night,
  Ere slumber's chain has bound me,
Fond memory brings the light
  Of other days around me;

The smiles, the tears of boyhood's years,
    The words of love then spoken.
The eyes that shone, now dimmed and gone,
    The cheerful hearts now broken.
        Thus in the stilly night, &c.

When I remember all
    The friends so linked together,
I've seen around me fall
    Like leaves in winter weather;
I feel like one who treads alone,
    Some banquet hall deserted,
Whose lights are fled, whose garland's dead,
    And all but he departed.
        Thus in the stilly night, &c.

------◆◆◆------

Will You Come to the Bower?

Will you come to the bower I have shaded for you?
Our bed shall be roses bespangled with dew.
    Will you, will you, will you, will you come to the
        bower?

There under the bower on roses you lie,
With a blush on your cheek, but a smile in your eye.
    Will you, will you, will you, will you smile my
        beloved?

But the roses we press shall not rival your lip,
Nor the dew be so sweet as the kisses we'll sip.
    Will you, will you, will you, will you kiss me my
        love?

And oh! for the joys that are sweeter than dew,
From languishing roses, or kisses from you.
    Will you, will you, will you, will you, won't you
        my love?

Happy Land of Canaan.

I sing you a song, and it won't detain me long,
  All about the times we are gaining;
I sing it in rhymes, and suit it to the times,
  And call it the happy land of Canaan.

CHORUS :—Oh! oh! oh! ah! ah! ah!—
Look out, there's a good time coming;
Never mind the weather, but get over double trouble,
I am bound for the happy land of Canaan.

Old Abe Lincoln was elected President,
  And from a rail-splitter he is gaining;
The Yankees they may brag, but we'll raise the flag,
  And make the South a happy land of Canaan.

CHORUS :—Oh! oh! oh! ah! ah! ah! &c.

Down at Harper's Ferry section they raised an insur-
    rection,
  Old Brown thought the nigger would sustain him,
Along came Governor Wise, and took him by surprise,
  And sent him to the happy land of Canaan.

CHORUS :—Oh! oh! oh! ah! ah! ah! &c.

Old Brown is dead, and the last word he said
  Was, don't keep me here long remaining;
First we took him up a slope, then dropped him on a
    rope,
And dropped him in the happy land of Canaan.

CHORUS ;—Oh! oh! oh! ah! ah! ah! &c.

Old Buchanan got his orders, and left the 4th of March,
  And says some credit he was gaining;
Good folks let him rest, the old man has done his best,
  He is bound for the happy land of Canaan.

CHORUS :—Oh! oh! oh! ah! ah! ah! &c.

Now Jeff. Davis shakes his fists at the Abolitionists,
  And says he would give them a training;
He would hang them so freely, both Smith and Horace
    Greely,
  If he could catch them in the happy land of Canaan.
CHORUS :—Oh! oh! oh! ah! ah! ah! &c.

The Three Rogues who Couldn't Sing.

In good old Colony times,
  When we lived under the King,
Three roguish chaps fell into mishaps
  Because they could not sing.

CHORUS :—Because they could not sing,
  Because they could not sing;
Three roguish chaps fell into mishaps
  Because they could not sing.

The first he was a miller,
  The second he was a weaver,
And the third he was a little tai-lor,
  Three roguish chaps together.

CHORUS :—Three roguish chaps together, &c.

The miller he stole corn,
  The weaver he stole yarn,
And the little tai-lor stole broadcloth for
  To keep these three rogues warm.

CHORUS :—To keep these three rogues warm, &c.

The miller was drowned in his dam,
  The weaver was hung in his yarn,
And the devil clapp'd his claw on the little tai-lor,
  With his broadcloth under his arm.

CHORUS :—With his broadcloth under his arm,·
  With his broadcloth under his arm;
And the devil clapp'd his claw on the little tai-lor,
  With his broadcloth under his arm.

Stonewall Jackson's Way.

[The Boston Courier says : "The following stanzas were found on the person of a rebel sergeant of the 'Stonewall Brigade,' captured near Winchester, Va."]

Come, stack arms, men! pile on the rails,
  Stir up the camp fire bright,
No matter if the canteen fails,
  We'll make a roaring light.
Here Shenandoah brawls along,
The burly Blue Ridge echoes strong,
To swell the brigade's rousing song
  Of "Stonewall Jackson's way."

We see him now. the old slouched hat
  Cocked over his eyes askew,
The shrewd dry smile, the speech so pat,
  So calm, so blunt, so true.
The "Blue Light Elder" knows 'em well,
Says he, "That's Banks, he's fond of shell,
Lord save his soul! we'll give him"—well,
  That's "Stonewall Jackson's way."

Silence! ground arms, kneel all, caps off,
  Old Blue Light's going to pray :
Strangle the fool that dares to scoff—
  Attention! it's his way.
Appealing from his native sod
In *forma pauperis* to God,
"Lay bare thine arm, stretch forth thy rod,
  Amen!" That's "Stonewall's way."

He's in the saddle now. Fall in?
  Steady, the whole brigade;
Hill's at the ford cut off—we'll win
  His way out, ball and blade.
What matter if our shoes are worn?
What matter if our feet are torn?
"Quick step! we're with him before morn,"
  That's "Stonewall Jackson's way."

The sun's bright lances rout the mists
  Of morning, and, by George,
Here's Longstreet struggling in the lists,
  Hemmed in an ugly gorge.
Pope and his Yankees whipped before,
"Bay'nets and grape!" hear Stonewall roar;
"Charge, Stuart, pay off Ashby's score," •
  Is "Stonewall Jackson's way."

Ah! maiden, wait, and watch, and yearn,
  For news of Stonewall's band;
Ah! widow, read with eyes that burn,
  That ring upon thy hand.
Ah! wife, sew on, pray on, hope on,
Thy life shall not be all forlorn,
The foe had better ne'er been born
  That gets in "Stonewall's way."

———————————◆◆◆———————————

All Quiet Along the Potomac To-Night.

"All quiet along the Potomac," they say,
  "Except now and then a stray picket
Is shot as he walks on his beat to and fro
  By a rifleman hid in the thicket."
'Tis nothing: a private or two now and then
  Will not count in the news of the battle;
Not an officer lost, only one of the men,
  Moaning out all alone the death rattle.

All quiet along the Potomac to-night,
  Where the soldiers lie peacefully dreaming;
Their tents in the rays of the clear autumn moon,
  Or the light of the watch-fires, are gleaming.
A tremulous sigh as the gentle night wind
  Through the forest trees slowly is creeping,
While the stars up above, with their glittering eyes,
  Keep guard, for the army is sleeping.

There's only the sound of the lone sentry's tread
  As he tramps from the rock to the fountain,
And thinks of the two on the low trundle bed
  Far away in the cot on the mountain.

His musket falls slack, his face dark and grim,
  Grows gentle with memories tender,
As he mutters a prayer for his children asleep—
  For their mother—may Heaven defend her.

The moon seems to shine as brightly as then,
  That night when the love yet unspoken
Leaped up to his lips, and when low murmured vows
  Were pledged to be ever unbroken.
Then drawing his sleeves roughly over his eyes,
  He dashes off tears that are swelling,
And gathers his gun close up to its place,
  As if to keep down the heart's welling.

He passes the fountain, the blasted pine-tree,
  The footstep is lagging and weary,
Yet onward he goes, through the broad belt of light,
  Towards the shades of a forest so dreary.
Hark! was it the night wind that rustled the leaves?
  Was it the moonlight, so wondrously flashing?
It looked like a rifle—ha! Mary, good-bye,
  And the life-blood is ebbing and splashing.

All quiet along the Potomac to-night,
  No sound save the rush of the river,
While soft falls the dew on the face of the dead—
  The picket's off duty forever.

------◆◆◆------

Old Cabin Home.

  I am going far away,
  Far away to leave you now,
To the Mississippi river I am going;
  I will take my old banjo,
  And I'll sing this little song,
'Way down in my old cabin home.

CHORUS—Here is my old cabin home,
      Here is my sister and my brother,
      Here lies my wife, the joy of my life,
        And my child in the grave with its mother.

2

When old age comes on,
And my hair is turning grey,
I will hang up the banjo all alone,
I'll sit down by the fire,
And I'll pass the time away,
'Way down in my old cabin home.

Chorus—There is my old cabin home, &c.

'Tis there where I roam,
'Way down on de old farm
Where all the darkies are free;
Oh! merrily sound the banjo
For de white folks round de room,
'Way down in my old cabin home.

Chorus—Here is my old cabin home, &c.

Rock Me to Sleep.

Backward, turn backward, O Time, in your flight,
Make me a child again just for to-night.
Mother, come back from the echoless shore,
Take me again to your heart as of yore;
Kiss from my forehead the furrows of care,
Smooth the few silver threads out of my hair,
Over my slumbers your loving watch keep,
Rock me to sleep, mother, rock me to sleep.

Backward, flow backward, O tide of years,
I am so weary of toils and of tears:
Toil without recompense, tears all in vain,
Take them, and give me my childhood again.
I have grown weary of dust and decay,
Weary of flinging my soul-wealth away:
Weary of sowing for others to reap,
Rock me to sleep, mother, rock me to sleep.

Tired of the hollow, the base, the untrue,
Mother, O mother, my heart calls for you.
Many a summer the grass has grown green,
Blossomed and faded, our faces between.

Yet with strong yearning and passionate pain
Long 1 to-night for your presence again;
Come from your silence so long and so deep,
Rock me to sleep, mother, rock me to sleep.

Over my heart in days that are flown,
No love like mother-love ever has shone,
No other worship abides and endures,
Faithful, unselfish, and patient like yours;
None like mother can charm away pain
From the sick soul and the world-weary brain;
Slumber's soft calm o'er my heavy lids creep,
Rock me to sleep, mother, rock me to sleep.

Come, let your brown hair, just lighten'd with gold,
Fall on your shoulders again as of old,
Let it fall over my forehead to-night,
Shading my faint eyes away from the light;
For with its sunny-edged shadows once more
Happily will throng the sweet visions of yore,.
Lovingly, softly, its bright billows sweep,
Rock me to sleep, mother, rock me to sleep.

Mother, dear mother, the years have been long
Since I last hushed to your lullaby song;
Sing then, and unto my soul it shall seem
Womanhood's years have been but a dream;
Clasp to your arms in a loving embrace,
With your light lashes just sweeping my face,
Never hereafter to wake or to weep,
Rock me to sleep, mother, rock me to sleep.

————◆●◆————

Mary.

Come, draw thee near my elbow chair,
  My dainty little Mary;
And, while your needles tic tac there,
Upon your forehead, once so fair,
I, with a one-and-twenty air,
  Shall plant a kiss, my Mary.

Shall plant a kiss, and bid it grow
    So rosily—my Mary—
So star-like on that arch of snow—
That milky-way of thought which so
Won all worship long ago,
    My heart of hearts, my Mary!

Oh! 'tisn't winters makes us old,
    My little merry Mary:
Your heart has neither blight nor cold,
Although your brow, of queenly mould,
They say, has changed its rippling gold
    For sober silver, Mary.

Ha!—On my cheeks and through my brain
    What music trips there, Mary,
More witching than when summer rain
Plays tip-tap on the whitening grain?
That hand—ha, ha! 'tis there again—
    Thy gleeful hand, my Mary.

Oh! Mary—Mary, gay and mild—
    My dearest, dearest Mary,
I hear your laughter, warm and mild,
And feel once more a little child,
My love—my dove—my undefiled,
    My sun—my moon—my Mary.

Gideon's Band.

Oh! keep your hat upon your head,
Oh! keep your hat upon your head,
Oh! keep your hat upon your head,
For you will want it when you're dead.
CHORUS—If you belong to Gideon's band,
    Oh! here's my heart and here's my hand;
    If you belong to Gideon's band,
    We're hunting for a home.

Oh! keep your nose upon your face,
Oh! keep your nose upon your face,
Oh! keep your nose upon your face,
For anywhere else 'tis out of place.
If you belong, etc.

Oh! keep your pants upon your legs,
Oh! keep your pants upon your legs,
Oh! keep your pants upon your legs,
That you may hang 'em on the golden pegs.
If you belong, etc.

Oh! stick your toe-nails in the ground,
Oh! stick your toe-nails in the ground,
Oh! stick your toe-nails in the ground,
That when you're wanted you may be found.
If you belong, etc.

'Twixt you and I, I really think,
'Twixt you and I, I really think,
'Twixt you and I, I really think,
It's pretty near time to take a drink.
If you belong, etc.

Oh! keep your coat upon your back,
Oh! keep your coat upon your back,
Oh! keep your coat upon your back,
That you may be off on the other track.
If you belong, etc.

Oh! keep your shoes upon your feet,
Oh! keep your shoes upon your feet,
Oh! keep your shoes upon your feet,
That you may walk in the golden street.
If you belong, etc.

Oh! keep your money in your pocket,
Oh! keep your money in your pocket,
Oh! keep your money in your pocket,
So when it's wanted you've not forgot it.
If you belong, etc.

ADDITIONAL VERSES.

Eve she did an apple pull,
Eve she did an apple pull,
Eve she did an apple pull,
And then she filled her apron full.
    If you belong, etc.

Then Adam did a small piece take,
Then Adam did a small piece take,
Then Adam did a small piece take,
And it gave him the belly-ache.
    If you belong, etc.

The devil he did come around,
The devil he did come around,
The devil he did come around,
And saw the peelings on the ground.
    If you belong, etc.

Then Adam came to her relief,
Then Adam came to her relief,
Then Adam came to her relief,
All dressed up in a new Fig leaf.
    If you belong, etc.

Old Noah he did build an ark,
Old Noah he did build an ark,
Old Noah he did build an ark,
He built it out of Hickory bark.
    If you belong, etc.

When from the ark he did get free,
When from the ark he did get free,
When from the ark he did get free,
He went upon a high old spree.
    If you belong, etc.

When Noah did get through his spree,
When Noah did get through his spree,
When Noah did get through his spree,
He banished Ham to Africa.
    If you belong, etc.

Oh! chase the devil round the stump,
Oh! chase the devil round the stump,
Oh! chase the devil round the stump,
And hit him a crack upon his ——.
    If you belong, &c.

Remember, Love, Remember.

'Twas ten o'clock, one moonlight night,
  I ever shall remember,
And every star shone sparkling bright
  In gloomy cold December,
When at my window, tap, tap, tap,
I heard his gentle well known rap,
  And with it, too, these words most clear,
  'Remember ten o'clock, my dear,
Remember, love, remember.'

Now mam sat dozing by the fire,
  And dad his pipe was smoking,
I dare not for the world retire,
  And was not that provoking?
At last the old folks fell asleep,
I hasten'd my promised vow to keep;
  But he his absence to denote,
  Had on the window shutter wrote,
'Remember, love, remember.'

But did I need the hint so sweet?
  No, no, for mark the warning,
Which meant that we at church should meet
  At ten o'clock next morning.
And there we met, no more to part,
There joined together hand and heart;
  And since that day in wedlock joined,
  The window shutter brings to mind,
Remember, love, remember.

Cora Lee.

Years have flown since last I saw thee,
   Standing in thy cottage door,
But thy smiles are ever near me,
   Though I see thee never more;
See the willow sways the tresses
   O'er thy grave, dear Cora Lee,
And at eve the dew drop nestles
   In the wild flowers over thee.

CHORUS—Pale the moonbeams fall at evening,
      On the green turf over thee;
      But thy gentle soul's in Heaven,
      Farewell, lost one, Cora Lee.

Ringlets bright as golden sunbeams,
   Floating o'er thy pale young brow,
And a form whose fancy fair dreams
   Ne'er can bring us one like thou.
No pale marble gleams above thee,
   Yet how dear that spot to me;
Memory whispers still I love thee,
   Angel stolen, Cora Lee.

CHORUS—Pale the moonbeams, &c.

Now thy voice, like music stealing,
   Lingers round where last we met,
And I hear thee while I'm sleeping,
   Whisper, thou canst ne'er forget.
See, the willow sways its tresses
   O'er thy grave, dear Cora Lee,
And at eve the dew drop nestles
   In the wild flowers over thee.
CHORUS—Pale the moonbeams, &c.

A Life on the Ocean Wave.

A life on the ocean wave,
   A home on the rolling deep,
Where the scattered waters rave,
   And the winds their revels keep.

Like an eagle caged I pine
　On this dull, unchanging shore,
Oh !ᵊgive me the flashing brine,
　The spray and the tempest's roar.

Once more on the deck I stand
　Of my own swift gliding craft;
Set sail, farewell to the land,
　The gale follows far abaft.
We shoot through the sparkling foam,
　Like an ocean bird set free;
Like the ocean bird, our home
　We'll find far out on the sea.

The land is no longer in view,
　The clouds have begun to frown,
But with a stout vessel and crew
　We'll say let the storms come down;
And the song of our hearts shall be,
　While the wind and the waters rave,
A life on the heaving sea,
　A home on the bounding wave.

--- ---- ◆●◆ ----- ----

'Paddy Whack, or the Bould Soulger.

Och ! I'm Paddy Whack; from Balle-na-hack,
　Not long ago turned soulger,
And to storm the attack, the grand attack,
　There's none than I'll be boulder.
With spirit gay we marched away
　To see each fair behoulder,
And the ladies all cry, it's me they spy,
　'Oh ! what a lovely soulger.'
　　In Londonderry, in London merry,
　　　We lived, dear girls, to charm ye,
And down ye'll come, when we rattle the drum,
　To see us in the armye.

Och! there's lots of girls me trade unfurls,
  Who'd form a dacent party,
There's Peggy Lynch, a tidy wench,
  And Sue and Ann McCarthy;
And Julia Biaggs, and Martha Scraggs,
  And Mollie Snaggs, all stormie,
And Mistress White, who's lost her sight,
  She admires me in the armye.
    In Londonderry, in London merry, &c.

And if I go on as I begun,
  My comrades all inform me,
It's their belafe, Commander-in-chafe
  I soon will be in the armye.
    In Londonderry, in London merry, &c.

Eulalie.

Blue birds linger here awhile,
O'er this sacred gra sy pile;
Sing your sweete-t songs to me—
'Tis the grave of Eulalie.
Roses white, around her tomb,
Gently wave and sweetly bloom;
Let your silent language be,
'We will bloom for Eulalie.'

Streamlet, chanting at her feet,
Mournful music, sad and sweet,
Wake her not, she dreams of me
'Neath the yew-tree. Eulalie!
Eulalie, but yesternight
Came a spirit vailed in white;
I knew it could be none but thee,
Bride of death, lost Eulalie.

Angels, guard her with your wings,
Shield her from unholy things;
Bid her dream love-dreams of me—
Till I come, sleep, Eulalie!

Blue birds linger here awhile,
O'er this sacred grassy pile;
Sing your sweetest songs to me,
'Tis the grave of Eulalie.

Charity.

Meek and lowly, pure and holy,
  Chief among the blessed three,
Turning sadness into gladness,
  Heaven born art thou, Charity!
Pity dwelleth in thy bosom;
  Kindness reigneth o'er thy heart;
Gentle thoughts alone can sway thee;
  Judgment hath in thee no part.

Hoping ever, failing never;
  Though deceived, believing still;
Long abiding, all confiding,
  To thy Heavenly Father's will;
Never weary of well-doing,
  Never fearful of the end;
Claiming all mankind as brothers,
  Thou dost all alike befriend.

Annie, We Have Parted.

AIR—'Willie, We Have Missed You.'

Oh! Annie, we have parted, my happy dream is o'er;
I leave thee broken-hearted, to meet, perchance no
    more.
The world looks not so bright, love, as once it did to
    me;
'Tis shrouded now in night, love, for I am leaving
    thee;
And yet your voice seems sweeter, your song is still as
    glad;
Oh! Annie, we have parted, and now my heart is
    sad.

I never can forget thee, though years may pass away,
The time when first I met thee, a lovely Summer
    day;
The vows that once were spoken, upon that Summer's
    eve,
Shall they remain unbroken, can my poor heart be-
    lieve?
But you say that we have parted, and my every thought
    is vain;
Oh! Annie, we have parted, and ne'er shall meet
    again.

The hopes that I would cherish, I'll banish from my
    heart,
I'll let each fond dream perish, since you and I must
    part;
The hours once filled with gladness, are fraught with
    sorrow now;
My heart is sick with sadness, 'tis marked upon my
    brow;
I leave thee in thy beauty, and yet 'tis sad, with
    pain;
Oh! Annie, we have parted, and ne'er shall meet
    again.

Oh! Annie, we have parted, and I again must find
Another, more true-hearted, one gentle and more
    kind;
And when afar I roam, love, across the trackless sea,
Far from my native home, love, I'll still remember
    thee,
And each fond thought will linger around my weary
    heart;
Oh! Annie, I have loved thee, 'tis sadness now to
    part.

———◆●◆———

'Mr. Johnson, did you eber see dat wire bridge at
Nigger Falls?' 'Oh, yes, last summer. Wonder what
dat cost?' 'Don't know, Johnson; if you cross ober
you'll be toll'd.'

Thou Hast Wounded the Spirit.

Thou hast wounded the spirit that loved thee,
And cherished thine image for years;
Thou hast taught me at last to forget thee,
In secret, in silence, in tears;
As a young bird, when left by its mother,
Its earliest pinions to try,
'Round the nest will still lingering hover,
Ere its trembling wings can fly.

Thus we're taught in this cold world to smother
Each feeling that once was so dear;
Like that young bird, I'll seek to discover
A home of affection elsewhere.
Tho' this heart may still cling to thee fondly,
And dream of sweet memories past,
Yet Hope, like the rainbow of summer,
Gives a promise of Lethe at last.

My Love, He is a Salieur Boy.

Oh, my love, he is a salieur boy, so gal-li-ent and
bold;
He is straight as any flag-staff, only nineteen years
old;
For to cruise the wide o-shi-en, he's left his own
dear,
And my heart it is a bus-ti-en, because he isn't here.

CHORUS.

For his spirit was tremen-du-us and fierce to behold,
For a young man bred a carpenter, only nineteen years
old.

His pa-ri-ents tney bounded him, all for to be a carpenter,
But a sea-farin' life he did very much prefer,

For his spirit was tremen-du-us and fierce to behold,
For a young man bred a carpenter, only nineteen years
    old.
    For his spirit was tremen-du-us, etc.

Oh, my bosom it is tos-ti-ed, just like the raging sea,
For fear that his affec-shi-uns don't still pint to me;
For a lovyer can be found in each port, I am told,
Especially for a young man only nineteen years old.
    For his spirit was tremen-du-us, etc.

And if my dear hus-bi-end he never will be,
But lay a cold corpus in the bottom of the sea;
Oh, the weeds of a widow, so dismi-el to behold,
I would wear for my salieur boy, only nineteen years
    old.
    For his spirit was tremen-du-us, etc.

And it's oh, for my lovyer I grieve and repine,
For fear that this young man will never be mine;
All the wealth of the In-di-es, in silvyer and colat-
    ariel,
I'd give for my salieur boy, only nineteen years old.
    For his spirit was tremen-du-us, etc.

Der Bold Privateer.

Oh, my dearest Polly, you and I must part,
I'm goin' across der seas, loov, I gif to you my heart;
My ship she lies in vaiting, so fare dee vell my dear,
I am shust a goin' on board of der bold Privateer.
    Und der bold Privateer, und der bold Privateer;
    I am shust a goin' on board of der bold Privateer.

But, oh, my dearest Shonny, great dangers have been
    crossed,
And many a sweet life by der seas has been lost.

'ou had petter sthop to home mit ter girl vat loovs
    you dear,
'han to venture your sweet life oñ de bold Privateer.
Und der bold Privateer, und der bold Privateer;
You is shust goin' on board of der bold Privateer.

'en der wars is over, I hopes dey vill spare my life;
)en soon I vill come back agin to my loovin' wile;
)en soon I vill git marred to sharming Polly dear,
ind den I'll bid goot bye to der bold Privateer.
Und der bold Privateer, und der bold Privateer,
I am shust a goin' on board of der bold Privateer.

ih! my dearest Polly, your friends don't me like;
esides, youse got two brothers, who'd quickly take
    my life;
ome, change your rings mit me, my love—come,
    change your rings mit me,
nd dat -hall be our token ven I am on der sea.
Und der bold Privateer, und der bold Privateer,
I am shust a goin' on board of der bold Privateer.

Larry O'Brien.

I've just returned from the ocean,
Where thunder and ball are in motion,
For fighting I've niver had a notion,
It would never do for Larry O'Brien.
ve boxed along the shore, like a great many more,
ve knocked down the spalpeens by the half score;
ut I niver thought it clivei, for the balls to knock the
    liver
ut of Larry, Larry, young Larry.
Oh! the divil take the girl wouldn't have me,
    wouldn,t have me, wouldn't have me,
The divil take the girl wouldn't have me,
She'd niver do for Larry O'Brien.

There's a dirty little middy in the milk shop,
Faith! he ordered me up to the maintop,
And my head swam around like a whip-top,
'Twas no place for Larry O'Brien.
The sailors up above they let down a rope,
They tied it round my waist, and they hauled me up,
And I kept a bawling and a squawling,
But the divils they kept a hauling
Of Larry, Larry, Larry, young Larry.
  Oh! the divil take, &c.

   While this hullabuloo they all were a making,
   I lay in the hold shivering and shaking,
   Till I heard the French ship-of-war taking,
   Then out-popped Larry O'Brien.
The first thing I saw was a man lying dead,
Says I, ·Sir, 'pon my soul, you had better been in bed,
Than be delighting in such fighting,'
Which I thought was no ways inviting
     To Larry, &c.

   Now the Captain gave orders for a sailing,
   But the sides of our ship wanted nailing;
   All hands to the pumping and bailing,
   There was work for Larry O'Brien.
With their hammers and their blocks, and their mighty
    heavy knocks,
She looked for all the world like the divil in the
    clocks,
And with their oakum, the divil choke 'em,
And they had for to poke 'em
     On to Larry, &c.

   Now I'll bid adieu to the Captain and the sailors,
   Likewise to the caulkers and the bailers,
   And I'll start right off for the tailors,
   For to rig out young Larry O'Brien.
And then, blood an' ouns, when I'm free from all
    wounds,
I'll marry some plump widdy, worth twenty thousand
    pounds,

I'll adore her, and get down on my knees before her,
And implore her for to marry
   Young Larry, &c.

------◆◆◆------

I'll Tell Nobody.

Oh! I am in love, but I won't tell with who,
  For I know very well what the fair ones would do,
They'd chatter, and flutter, and make themselves fine,
  So poor little some one would have a sad time.
So I'll tell nobody, I'll tell nobody, nobody, nobody,
  nobody, no.

If I tell it to one, she will tell it to two;
  At the next cup of tea they would plot what to do;
And as man no constancy have in their own mind,
  He'd seek a new face, and leave some one behind.
So I'll tell nobody, &c.

But this much I'll tell you, he is not over tall,
  And lest you should guess him, he's not very small;
I met him last night, and he pulled off my glove,
  So I think you may guess who is somebody's love.
But I'll tell nobody, &c.

But when I am sure that his heart's all my own,
  That he loves sincerely, and never will roam;
Oh! then I'll defy all their jeers and their taunts,
  For plainly 'twill show what 'tis each of them
    wants;
  They all want somebody—are dying for somebody,
    somebody, somebody, I know who.

------◆◆◆------

Maggie By My Side.

The land of my home is flitting, flitting from my view;
A gale in the sail is sitting, toils the merry crew,
Here let my home be on the waters wide,
I roam with a proud heart—Maggie's by my side.

CHORUS—My own loved Maggie, dear,
    Sitting by my side;
    Maggie, dear, my own love,
    Sitting by my side.

The wind howling o'er the billow from the distant
    lea,
The storm raging round my pillow brings no care to
    me;
Roll on ye dark waves o'er the troubled tide,
I heed not your anger—Maggie's by my side.
    My own loved Maggie, dear, &c.

Storms can appal me never while her brow is clear,
Fair weather lingers ever where her smiles appear;
When sorrow's breakers 'round my heart shall hide,
Still may I find her sitting by my side.
    My own loved Maggie, dear, &c.

————————◆◆————————

The Young Recruit.

See! there's ribbons gaily streaming,
    I'm a soldier now, Lizette;
Yes, of battles I am dreaming,
    And the honor I shall get.
With a sabre by my side,
    And a helmet on my brow,
And a proud steed to ride,
    I shall rush on the foe.
Yes, I flatter me, Lizette,
    'Tis a life that will suit
The gay life of a young recruit.

We will march away to-morrow
    At the breaking of the day,
And the trumpets will be sounding,
    And the merry cymbals play;
Yet before I say good-bye,
    And a last sad parting take,

As a proof of your love
Wear this gift for my sake.
Then cheer up. my own Lizetta,
Let not your grief your beauty stain,
Soon you'll see the young recruit again.

------◆◆◆------

The Drinking Song.

[FROM LUCRETIA BORGIA.]

It is better to laugh than be sighing,
When we think how life's moments are flying,
For each sorrow fate ever is bringing,
There is a pleasure in store for us springing,
'Tho' our joys, like waves in the sunshine,
Gleam awhile, then be lost to sight;
 Yet for each sparkling ray,
 That so passes away,
Comes another so brilliant and bright.

 Then 'tis better to laugh than be sighing,
  They are wise who resolve to be gay,
 When we think how life's moments are flying,
  Oh! enjoy pleasure's gifts while we may.

In the world we some beings discover,
Far too frigid for friend or for lover;
Souls.unblest, and forever repining,
'Tho' good fortune around them be shining.
It were well if such hearts we could banish,
To some planet far distant from ours;
 They are the dark spots we trace
 On this earth's favored space,
They are weeds that choke up the fair flowers.

 Then 'tis better to laugh than be sighing,
  They are wise who resolve to be gay,
 When we think how life's moments are flying,
  Oh! enjoy pleasure's gifts while we may.

Willie, We Have Missed You.

Oh! Willie, is it you, dear,
    Safe, safe at home;
They did not tell me true, dear,
    They said you would not come.
I heard you at the gate,
    And it made my heart rejoice,
For I knew that welcome footstep,
    And that dear familiar voice,
Making music on my ear,
    In the lonely midnight gloom;
Oh! Willie, we have missed you,
    Welcome, welcome home.

We've longed to see you nightly,
    But this night of all;
The fire was blazing brightly,
    And lights were in the hall.
The little ones were up,
    Till 'twas ten o'clock and past,
Then their eyes began to twinkle,
    And they've gone to sleep at last;
But they listened for your voice
    Till they thought you'd never come;
Oh! Willie, we have missed you,
    Welcome, welcome home.

The days were sad without you,
    The nights long and drear,
My dreams have been about you,
    Oh! welcome Willie, dear!
Last night I wept and watched
    By the moonlight's cheerless ray,
Till I thought I heard your footstep,
    Then I wiped my tears away;
But my heart grew sad again
    When I found you had not come;
Oh! Willie, we have missed you,
    Welcome, welcome home.

Faded Flowers.

The flowers that I saw in the wildwood
Have since drooped their beautiful leaves,
And the many dear friends of my childhood
Have slumbered for years in their graves.
Oh! the bloom of the flowers I remember,
But the faces I never more shall see,
For the cold chilly winds of December
Stole my flowers, my companions from me.

The roses may bloom on the morrow,
And many a friend have I won;
Yet my heart will bow down with its sorrow,
When I think how the loved ones are gone.
'Tis no wonder that I'm broken hearted,
And stricken with sorrow should be,
We have met, we have loved, we have parted,
My flowers, my companions and me.

How dark looks this world, and how dreary,
When we think of the ones that we love,
Yet there's rest for the faint and the weary,
When friends meet with lost ones above.
Yet in heaven I can but remember,
When from earth my proud soul shall be free;
Then no cold chilly winds of December
Can part my companions and me.

The Original Dixie.

I wish I was in the land of cotton,
Old times dar am not forgotten.
Look away—look away—look away—Dixie Land.
In Dixie Land whar I was born in,
Early on one frosty mornin',
Look away—look away—look away—Dixie Land.

Den I wish I was in Dixie,
    Hooray! Hooray!
In Dixie Land I'll took my stand,
To lib an' die in Dixie
    Away, away, away down South in Dixie.
    Away, away, away down South in Dixie.

Old missus marry 'Will de-weaber,'
William was a gay deceaber.
Look away, &c.
    But when he put his arm around 'er,
    He smiled as fierce as a forty pounder.
Look away, &c.
    Den I wish I was in Dixie, &c.

His face was sharp as a butcher's cleaber,
But dat did not seem to grieb 'er.
Look away, &c.
    Old missus acted de foolish part,
    And died for the man that broke her heart.
Look away, &c.
    Den I wish I was in Dixie, &c.

Now here's a health to the next old missus,
And all the gals that want to kiss us.
Look away, &c.
    But if you want to drive 'way sorrow,
    Come and hear dis song to-morrow.
Look away, &c.
    Den I wish I was in Dixie, &c.

Dars buckwheat cakes and Ingun batter,
Makes you fat, or a little fatter.
Look away, &c.
    Den hoe it down an' scratch your grabble,
    To Dixie's land I'm bound to trabble.
Look away, &c.
    Den I wish I was in Dixie, &c.

------◆◆◆------

When is a man not a man? When he's a shavin'.

Thinking of Thee.

I miss thee each lone hour,
　Star of my heart,
No other voice has power joy to impart;
　I listen for thy step,
Thy kind sweet tone, ᵗᴶ
　But silence whispers me,
Thou art alone.
　I listen for thy step,
Thy kind sweet tone,
　But silence whispers me,
Thou art alone.

Darkness is on the earth,
　Nought do I say;
Books are but little worth—
　Thou art away;
Voices, the true and kind,
　Strange are to me;
I have lost heart and mind
　Thinking of thee.
Voices, the true and kind,
　Strange are to me;
I have lost heart and mind
　Thinking of thee.

Her Bright Smile Haunts Me Still.

'Tis years since last we met,
　And we may not meet again;
I have struggled to forget,
　But the struggle was in vain,
For her voice lives on the breeze,
　And her spirit comes at will,
In the midnight, on the seas,
　Her bright smile haunts me still.

'Tis first sweet dawn of light,
    When I gaze upon the deep,
Her form still greets my sight,
    While the stars their vigils keep;
When I close mine aching eyes,
    Sweet dreams my senses fill,
And when from sleep I rise,
    Her bright smile haunts me still.

I have sail'd 'neath alien skies,
    I have trod the desert path,
I have seen the storm arise
    Like a giant in his wrath:
Every danger I have known,
    That a reckless life can fill,
Yet her presence is not flown,
    Her bright smile haunts me still.

--------◆◆◆--------

Farewell to the Star-Spangled Banner.

Let tyrants and slaves submissively tremble,
    And bow down their necks 'neath the Juggernaut
        car;
But brave men will rise in the strength of a nation,
    And cry give me freedom, or else give me war.

    Farewell for ever, the Star-spangled banner
    No longer shall wave o'er the land of the free;
    But we'll unfurl to the broad breeze of Heaven
    Thirteen bright stars round the Palmetto tree.

We honor, yes honor, bold South Carolina,
    Though small she may be, she's as brave as the best;
With flag-ship of State, she's out on the ocean
    Buffeting the waves of a dark biliow's crest.
        Farewell forever, &c.

We honor, yes honor, our seceding sisters,
 Who launched this brave bark alone on the sca;
Though storms may howl and thunder distraction,
 We'll hurl to the blast the proud Palmetto tree.
     Farewell forever, &c.

And when to the conflict the others cry onward,
 Virginia will be first to rush to the fight,
She'll break down the iceburg of Northern coercion,
 And rise in her glory of Freedom and right.
     Farewell forever, &c.

When the fifteen sisters in bright constellation,
 Shall dazzling shine in a nation's emblem sky;
With no hands to oppose, nor foes to oppress them,
 They will shine there forever, a light to every eye.
     Farewell forever, &c.

- --+-- ◆●◆--------

Wert Thou But Mine.

Wert thou but mine when morning lights the lea,
 And over lake and hill her glories shine;
My spirit waking, fondly flies to thee—
 My earliest wish is, ah, wert thou but mine!
          Wert thou but mine!

Wert thou but mine at midnight's hallowed hour,
 When all earth's weary ones from toil recline,
When guardian angels o'er thy pillow soar,
 In dreams I murmur, ah, wert thou but mine!
          Wert thou but mine!

Life may go roughly with me, foes may hate,
 Friends change, health fade, long cherished hopes
       decline,
Yet I could smile on all the shafts of fate,
 Wert thou but mine, beloved, wert thou but mine!
          Wert thou but mine!

Wert thou but mine, whatever fate befall,
  Howe'er in coming life my lot incline,
Thy love to light my path would brighten all,
  Wert thou but mine, beloved, wert thou but mine!
                  Wert thou but mine!

Allie Wayne.

'Twas in the early summer time,
  When earth seems all aglow,
When sun-beams smile the live-long day,
  And soft south breezes blow.
The flowers that slept through Winter's gloom
  Now rose as from the dead,
The warm sun kissed the dark, cold earth,
  Which blush'd in roses red.
  The flowers that slept through Winter's gloom, &c.

'Twas in this Summer, long ago, I met sweet Allie
      Wayne,
The glimpse of heaven she gave to me I ne'er shall
      see again;
Like flowers beguiled by young March winds, that op'd
      their buds too soon,
She came to me with Summer sweets, and died out
      with the June.
She came to me with Summer sweets, &c.

Ah! lonely yet ye are to me, sweet flowers, winds and
      streams,
Your memories glide o'er my soul like angels in our
      dreams;
Oh! golden days of Summer dead, will ye not come
      again?
Shall I not meet in brighter climes my angel Allie
      Wayne?
  Shall I not meet in brighter climes, &c.

'Sing and Rememder Me.'

Oh! sing this song when around thee gather,
  A faithful chos n few,
When thoughts are mingling with each other,
  And hearts beat warm and true
Oh! sing it when the pale stars glisten,
  Far o'er the waveless sea,
When zephyrs seem to stop and listen,
  Sing and remember me.

When sorrow o'er thy heart is stealing,
  And tears bedew thine eyes,
When twilight brings the hour of feeling,
  And stars tell destinies;
Then with thy soft and fairy finger
  Wake the string's melody;
Bid thoughts of other moments linger,
  Sing and remember me.

Pop Goes the Weasel.

King Abraham is very sick,
Old Scott has got the measles,
Manassas we have won at last—
    Pop goes the weasel!

All around the cobbler's house
The monkey chased the people,
And after them, in double haste,
    Pop went the weasel!

When the night walks in, as black as a sheep,
And the hen and her eggs were fast asleep,
When into her nest, with a serpent's creep,
    Pop went the weasel!

Of all the dance that ever was planned,
To galvanize the heel and the hand,
There's none that moves so gay and grand
    As pop goes the weasel!

Rory O'Moore.

BY SAMUEL LOVER.

Young Rory O'Moore courted Kathleen Bawn,
He was bold as the hawk, and she soft as the dawn,
He wished in his heart pretty Kathleen to please,
And he thought the best way to do that was to teaze.
'Now Rory be aisy,' sweet Kathleen would cry,
Reproof on her lip, but a smile in her eye—
'With your tricks I don't know in truth what I'm
    about,
Faith! you've teased till I've put on my cloak inside
    out.'
'Oh! Jewel,' says Rory, 'that same is the way
You've thrated my heart this many a day,
And 'tis plazed that I am, and why not, to be sure?
For 'tis all for good luck,' says bold Rory O'Moore.

'Indeed, then,' says Kathleen, 'don't think of the like,
For I half gave a promise to soothering Mike;
The ground that I walk on he loves I'll be bound.'
Says Rory, 'I'd rather love you than the ground.'
'Now, Rory, I'll cry if you don't let me go,
Sure I'm draming each night that I'm hating you so!'
Says Rory, 'that same I'm delighted to hear,
For drames always go by contraries, my dear.
Oh! darling, keep draming that same till you die,
And bright morning will give dirty night the black lie,
And 'tis plazed that I am, and why not, to be sure?
For 'tis all for good luck,' says bold Rory O'Moore.'

'Arrah! Kathleen, my darlint, you've tazed me
    enough,
And I've thrashed for your sake Dinny Grimes and
    Jem Duff;
And I've made myself drinking your health quite a
    haste,
So I think after that I may talk to the priest.'
Then Rory, the rogue, stole his arm round her neck,
So soft and so white, without freckle or speck;

And he looked in her eyes that were beaming with
    light,
And he kissed her sweet lips.   Don't you think he was
    right?
'Now, Rory, leave off, sir, you'll hug me no more,   ·
That's eight times to-day you have kissed me before '
'Then here goes another,' said he, to be sure.
'For there's luck in odd numbers,' says Rory O'Moore.'

Whistle, and I'll Come to You, my Lad.

Oh! whistle and I'll come to you my lad;
Oh! whistle, and I'll come to you my lad,
Though father and mother and all should go mad;
Oh! whistle, and I'll come to you my lad.

But warily tent when ye come to court me,
An' come na unless the back gate be a-ge,
Syne up the back style, and let nae body see,
And come as ye war nae coming to me.
              Oh! whistle, &c.

At kirk or at market whene'er ye meet me,
Go by me as though you cared na a flee,
But steal me a blink o' your bonny black ee,
Yet look as ye were na a looking at me.
              Oh! whistle, &c.

Ay, vow and protest that ye care nae for me,
And whiles ye may lightly my beauty awee,
But court na anither, though joking ye be,
For fear that she wiles your fancy frae me.
              Oh! whistle, &c.

'Twilight Dews.

When twilight dews are falling fast
    Upon the rosy sea,
I watch that star whose beams so oft
    Has lighted me to thee.

And thou, too, on that orb so dear,
 Ah! dost thou gaze at even,
And think, though lost forever here,
 Thou'lt yet be mine in heaven?
          And thou, too, on that, &c;

There's not a garden walk I tread,
 There's not a flower I see,
But brings to mind some hope that's fled,
 Some joy I've lost with thee;
And still I wish that hour was near,
 When friends and foes forgiven,
The pains, the ills we've wept through here,
 May turn to smiles in Heaven.

———————◆●◆———————

Irish Emigrant's Lament.

I'm sitting on the stile, Mary,
 Where we sat side by side,
On a bright May morning long ago,
 When first you were my bride;
The corn was springing fresh and green,
 And the lark sang loud and high,
And the red was on thy lip, Mary,
 And the love-light in thine eye.

The place is little changed, Mary,
 The day is bright as then,
The lark's loud song is in my ear,
 And the corn is green again!
But I miss the soft clasp of your hand,
 And your warm breath on my cheek,
And I still keep listening for the words
 You never more may speak.

'Tis but a step down yonder lane,
 And the little church stands near,
The church where we were wed, Mary,
 I see the spire from here.

But the graveyard lies between, Mary,
  And my step may break your rest,
For I've laid you, darling, down to sleep,
  With your baby on your breast.

I'm very lonely now, Mary,
  For the poor make no new friends;
But oh! they love them better far
  The few our Father sends;
And you were all I had, Mary,
  My blessing and my pride,
There's nothing left to care for now,
  Since my poor Mary died.

Yours was the brave, good heart, Mary,
  That still kept hoping on,
When the trust in God had left my soul,
  And my arm's young strength had gone.
There was comfort ever on your lip,
  And the kind look on your brow,
I bless you for that same, Mary,
  Though you can't hear me now.

Then You'll Remember Me.

When other lips and other hearts
  Their tale of love shall tell,
In language whose excess imparts
  The power they feel so well,
There may, perhaps, in such a scene
  Some recollection be
Of days that have as happy been,
  And you'll remember me,
And you'll remember, you'll remember me.

When coldness or deceit shall slight
  The beauty, now thy prize,
And deem it but a faded light,
  Which beams within your eyes.
When hollow hearts shall wear a mask,
  'Twill break your own to see,
In such a moment I but ask
  That you'll remember me,
And you'll remember, you'll remember me.

Down the River.

Oh! the river is up, and the channel is deep,
And the wind blows steady and strong,
Let the splash of your oars the measure keep,
As we row the old boat along.
Oh! the water is bright, and flashing like gold,
In the ray of the morning sun,
And old Dinah's away up out of the cold,
A getting the hoe cake done.
Oh! the river is up, and the channel is deep,
And the wind blows steady and strong,
Let the splash of your oars the measure keep,
As we row the old boat along.

CHORUS—Down the river, down the river,
Down the Ohio;
Down the river, down the river,
Down the Ohio.

[Chorus repeated.]

Oh! the master is proud of the old broad-horn,
For it brings him plenty of tin,
Oh! the crews they are darkies, the cargo is corn,
And the money comes tumbling in.
There's plenty on board for the darkies to eat,
And there's something to drink and to smoke,
There's the banjo, the bones, and the tambourine,
There's the song and the comical joke.
Oh! the river is up, and the channel is deep,
And the wind blows steady and strong,
Let the splash of your oars the measure keep,
As we row the old boat along. -

CHORUS—Down the river, &c.

[Chorus repeated.]

STONEWALL SONG BOOK.   69

I See Her Still in my Dreams.

While the flowers bloom in gladness, and spring-birds
   rejoice,
There's a void in our household of one gentle voice,
The form of a loved one has passed from the light,
But the sound of her footfall returned with the night;
   For I see her still in my dreams,
   I see her still in my dreams,
Though the light has departed from the meadows and
   streams,
   I see her still in my dreams.

Though her voice once familiar hath gone from the day,
And her smiles from the sunlight have faded away,
In my visions I find the lost form that I seek,
With light in her eye, and a blush on her cheek;
   For I see her still in my dreams,
   I see her still in my dreams,
Though her smiles have departed from the meadows
   and streams,
   I see her still in my dreams.

John Anderson, my Jo!

John Anderson, my Jo, John, when nature first began
To try her canny hand, John, her master-work was
   man;
And you among them a' John, so trig from top to toe,
She proved to be nae journey-work, John Anderson,
   my Jo !

John Anderson, my Jo, John, when we were first ac-
   quent,
Your locks were like the raven, your bonnie brow was
   brent;
But now your brow is bald, John, your locks are like
   the snow,
My blessings on your frosty-pow, John Anderson, my
   Jo!

John Anderson, my Jo, John, ye were my first conceit,
I think nae shame to own, John, I lo'ed ye ear and late.
They say ye're turning auld, John, and what though it
be so,
Ye're ay the same kind man to me, John Anderson,
my Jo!

John Anderson, my Jo, John, we've seen our bairns'
bairns,
And yet my dear John Anderson, I'm happy in your
arms,
And sae are ye in mine, John, I'm sure ye'll ne'er say
no,
Though the days are gane that we have seen, John
Anderson, my Jo!

John Anderson, my Jo, John, we clamb the hill thegither,
And mony a canty day, John, we've had w' ane
anither;
Now we maun totter down, John, but hand in hand
we'll go,
And sleep thegither at the foot, John Anderson, my Jo!

Was my Brother in the Battle?

Tell me, tell me, weary soldier, from the rude and
stirring wars,
Was my brother in the battle where you gained those
noble scars?
He was ever brave and valiant, and I know he never
fled,
Was his name among the wounded or numbered with
the dead?
Was my brother in the battle when the tide of war ran
high?
You would know him in a thousand by his dark and
flashing eye.
Tell me, tell me, weary soldier, will he never come
again,
Did he suffer 'mid the wounded or die among the slain?

Kingdom Coming.

Say, darkies, hab you seen ole massa
  Wid de muffstach on his face,
Go down de road some time dis morning,
  Like he gwine to leave de place?
He seen a smoke, way up de ribber, ,
  Whar de Link-um gunboats lay;
He took his hat, an' lef berry sudden,
  An' I spec he's run away.

CHORUS.

De massa run, ha! ha !
  De Darkey stay, ho! ho!
It must be now, de kingdom am a coming,
  An' de year ob ju-bi-lo!

He six foot one way, two foot tudder,
  An' he weigh four hundred pound;
His coat so big, he couldn't pay de tailor,
  An' it won't go half way round.
He drill so much, dey call him captain,
  An' he get so drefful tanned,
I spec he try to fool dem Yankees,
  For to tink he's con-tra-band.

CHORUS—De massa run, ha! ha! etc.

De darkies feel so lonesome,
  In de log-house on de lawn;
Dey move dar tings to massa's parlor
  For to keep it while he's gone.
Dars wine an' cider in de kitchen,
  An' de darkies dey'll hab some;
I spec's dey'll be con-fis-cat-ed,
  When de Link-um sojers come.

CHORUS—De massa run, ha! ha! etc.

INDEX.

www.ingramcontent.com/pod-product-compliance
Lightning Source LLC
Chambersburg PA
CBHW021529270326
41930CB00008B/1166